PIECES OF THE MOON

Stephen Brooke

Arachis Press 2011

Although I have, it seems, been writing poetry forever, *Pieces of the Moon* is my first book of poems. As such, this volume contains some of the best from the recent past. A few have been legitimate award winners, both in national and regional competitions.

Therefore, a variety of styles are represented. I have made no attempt to arrange them by date nor by technique; rather, I have endeavored to let one poem lead to the next through mood and subject. I hope you, the reader, enjoy this little sampler of my work.

Stephen Brooke, July 2003

©Stephen Brooke 2003
ISBN 978-1-937745-05-9

ARACHIS PRESS
4803 Peanut Road
Graceville, FL 32440
http://arachispress.com

PIECES OF THE MOON

A Bit of Moon

We have a bit of moon, tonight;
It shines its way into my bedroom,
Keeping me a while from sleep.
I should arise, slip from my covers,
Cross those cold floors, close those blinds
That I left open; blinds forgotten
When I made my drowsy round
Of locking doors and dimming lights.

It rose to shine, not long ago,
And now that moon lies on my bed,
Conversing of the day's events
Much like some lovers I have known.
At end of day comes lethargy;
This uninvited guest may stay.
It's late and I, in time, will sleep
So let the moon shine in, tonight.

APPLAUSE

Enter, stage left, our hero?
No, just a bit player
in an empty
auditorium. The cheers rise
silent from a darkened house
as he takes his bows and eats
his lunch. Encore?

GUITAR

a sijo

My guitars carry the names
of women I once knew.

Some I loved and some I might
have loved if life were different.

I play their memories each time
I hold one in my arms.

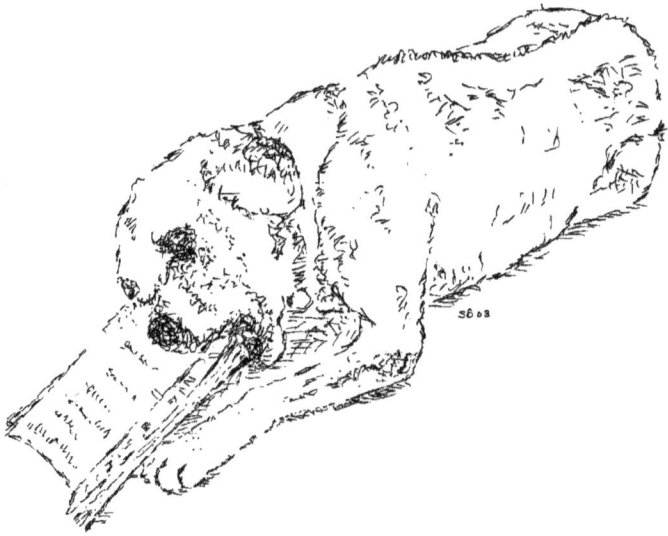

DOGS AND POETRY

All-day suckers, she called them;
one for each of her boys—
Donal, Mad Max, sleek Arrakis—
to gnaw when the long
Florida rains kept them indoors.

We were dogs and poetry,
she and I, dogs and poetry,
and I overlooked our mismatch
even as I did those marrow bones
scattered across her living room floor.

I've chewed the bones of us
long enough for all the flavor
to mix in uncertain memory
with the pleasures of some other time,
as her dogs have become my poetry.

It has stopped raining;
I want to run in the yard.

THIEF

I've picked Neruda's pocket,
lifted his wallet and spent
the words unwisely. I should
have given them to you.
Shall I snatch Sexton's purse
and buy you something nice?

Beggars

I have no truths to spare;
panhandle somewhere else.

My coat buttons all the way up
to keep out the cold.

Do the streets of heaven
lead anywhere?

What Gallows

I dance a jig upon the air
of never and forever more;

What gallows have I built of you,
that burns of memories and crows?

Cry not, my mother, 'twas my own
sweet crime that dangles me now so,

Between forgiveness and the time
of day. This rope sings me my pardon

In lullabies of melting sky,
in lullabies of melting sky.

THE KING OF SELF-PITY

Call me king:
ruler in my own nation,
my own little corner
of being.
King of self-pity,
king of that country
I built from memory
and broken hope.
Abdicate?
No, though ever so
attractive. The king
must face his execution,
head and crown
falling as one.
Walk with me once more;
give me a kiss goodbye
as I wave to the mob.

MY NAME

He knows me still; at least there's that.
His voice, become constant complaint,
Calls my name when the way from chair
To bathroom turns into a maze.

My poor ensorcelled knight is lost,
Is drawn by will-o-wisps away;
He now sees only mists and mirrors
And the faces of the dead.

I know he'll wander further yet
And some tomorrow may set out
With all his memories left in
My care, to never be reclaimed.

Then, when he loses even me,
I, too, shall count among the dead,
A ghost to hover helplessly,
One more of those forgotten faces.

I'm all that's left my faded boy,
My name his one familiar light:
The beacon that can draw him home,
Another day returned to me.

BENEDICTION

The wounds of our love
never heal; they sing
their stigmata across me,
a benediction of yearning.

Blessed be.

Blessed be
they who call the names
of lost love
in the night.

Blessed be
the broken hearted
for theirs is the kingdom
of yesterday.

Blessed be.

The faint scent
hangs in my eyes:
your incense burning,
burning yet.

INTERSTATES

Sixty-five, Seventy-five,
Ninety-five: the highways
that carried us away from home
to those jobs in Chicago,
Cleveland, Detroit. Hillbillies
on the assembly line. It beat
farming, beat working
in sweat-shop shirt factories,
afraid to unionize, knowing
the boss would pick up, pack up,
and move to Taiwan
or Thailand or some other
place we'll never see.
The signs are there, those red
and blue Interstate sirens
still sing, "Come on,
let's go home." But the Buick
stays in the drive. The kids
don't talk like us anymore
and the mortgage is half-paid
and I hear the old house was torn
down last year to make
room for a Seven-Eleven.

THE BLUES OF MY SOUL

In the dark rhythm of a rainy night,
when dreams drip from each branch of the live oaks,
the wind's a distant slide guitar
playing the blues of my soul.

Beyond the heat of this Southern summer dream,
lightning finds voice, growling a complaint
of lost love and forgetfulness
across the skies of then.

The world has become an empty room;
I called your name tonight and it was swallowed
by the darkness, by the rain,
by the blues of my soul.

HEEL

This song has no tune,
no words, only
the erratic beat
of your drum.
Let me remain thus
irrelevant,
inconvenient, holding
sparrows in
my open hand. This world
calls me old-fashioned;
should I wake up and smell
the century?

cont.

My beliefs are become
a secret lover
and my dog; I call
them to heel
but they ever pull
at the leash.
You think me weak for it,
your jealousy
will not let them run.
Let them run;
let them dig deep in search
of God's bones.

THREE DAYS, TWO NIGHTS

Doing my Anthony Newley shtick
for another middle-aged girl,
some twice-divorced chick with grandkids
and hair dye, cruising for number three
with Royal Caribbean; could it
be the guy with a bad toupee
who just bought her another drink,
while I tell her "It was a very good year,"
and for a moment she believes me?
Forget tonight, baldy, she'll be
another nameless port of call
for the lounge singer, always
on his way to Nassau and back,
in a powder-blue tux that carries the reek
of ten-thousand cigarettes
and the same forty songs.

The Whispered Songs

Twilit melancholy soft descends
upon a heart that will, yet troubled, yearn
for some forgotten love, not knowing why:
a shadowed memory of other lives,
the whispered songs no man can learn.

And, these dreams, they ever fade away,
though still along such paths my heart might turn,
perhaps to tarry, seeking to remember
all those many things I may not know,
the whispered songs I can not learn.

sB03

PIECES OF THE MOON

I am drunk with silken wine
laid soft upon the night;
oh, throw me pieces of the moon,
I'll fly them like a kite.

Cover me and I shall you
in skies of satin sheets,
as all the stars of heaven sail
away in morning's fleets.

Midnight's heady air pours out
its violet serenades;
oh, sing me pieces of the moon
before our zephyr fades.

Peripheral Vision

From a corner of my eye,
the silent room slides.
Ghosts, about ghostly business,
hover on the edge of the dust,
just beyond now.
Looking straight ahead will blind me;
one eye wakes, the other dreams.
It makes no difference
which is which.

I HAVE EATEN

I have eaten fresh, wet truth
plucked from your tree,
and found myself unsatisfied.
I'll sing away the taste;
no salt nor pepper
can make you palatable.

SIDESHOW #1

Step right this way, folks;
see the incredible man
with his head up his ass.
He thinks he lost yesterday
up there somewhere
but he'll shit it out
tomorrow morning,
as always.

SIDESHOW #2

Live girls here, gents,
real live,
drop dead
dancing girls,
dancing just for you.
Yes, gents,
only for you!
Please remain in your pants
at all times.

SHORT STUFF

She told me she was eighteen
but I sometimes wonder—
too young, too young.
Twice her age or thereabouts,
playing in a cover band
on the east side,
I'd step outside for a smoke
where the industrial park lights
leaked into the alley
over tenement roofs
and there she would be,
waiting.

cont.

For me? Maybe,
or maybe for any guy
who'd come out and put his arm
around her shoulders,
listen to her stories.
The usual shit—
abusive stepfather—
living with a friend—
could she have a smoke?
Maybe I could bring her out a beer?
Why don't I ever try anything with her?
She wouldn't mind.

No, Short Stuff, not me.
You find a job yet?
Don't make such a face, girl,
it wouldn't kill you—
better than giving blow jobs
over there behind the van.
Yeah, I've seen you—
hey, that's okay—
don't cry.

cont.

Then she wasn't there anymore;
gone back to Ohio,
the drummer told me—
too bad, he laughed—
she was a good little fuck.

Sorry 'bout the broken nose, dude.
You should have known better;
I should have known better.
Too many regrets—
too many shoulds and shouldn'ts
and I don't know what
became of her.
But I do still care enough
to wonder.

Sometimes.

TRAILER PARK

I lived alone, and baked French bread,
very crusty, in a trailer with
a leaky roof, every ten days.
The drips never bothered me that much—
My plants caught them and rent was cheap
at a dirt-road trailer park.

I worked odd jobs and subbed at school,
the classes no one else would take,
but I could always use the money
and Seven-Eleven wasn't hiring
art historians right then.
Mom wrote, *For this you got your degree?*

And if I didn't get a call
to teach shop or phys. ed. that day,
there would be waves to ride and pictures
to paint and I should learn that new
song for the latest short-lived band.
Yes, they sucked, but so did I.

cont.

Every day, I inched a bit
further from my youthful dreams;
every day, life seemed a bit
less worth living till the next
at a dirt-road trailer park
where rent was cheap and I lived alone.

WINDMILLS

Face it, she said,
you're just Don-fucking-Quixote
mistaking me for Dulcinea.
Go find another
girl of your dreams;
I don't want the job.
She left my world spinning
like windmills
on the plains of la Mancha.

SHRIMP CREOLE

Shrimp Creole, she promised;
I brought Chenin blanc—
no, not tart enough—
my old guitar, a head full of songs.

Arm around her in the moonlight,
I knew she wanted more,
something not within me that night.

Should I have pretended?
Should I have taken those lips
in hopes of rousing some sleeping passion?

Our roads now carry us apart,
and we'll forget that full moon night
when I sang for my supper.

STRING OF PEARLS

The big bands were hot
and so was the night
Glen Miller played
at Buckeye Lake.
You know the lake?
No, I guess
you wouldn't, wouldn't
know the amusement park
lights shining
across the water
as "String of Pearls"
filled the night.

cont.

She always said
they fell in love,
dancing there
beneath the stars
and the flashing signs
and the ferris wheel,
spinning slowly,
slowly in the heat
of an Ohio
summer night.

Sometimes, still,
those old swing songs
waken on the radio
and she dances across
the kitchen floor
with his memory,
as "String of Pearls"
fills the night.

WHO CAN SLEEP?

Who can sleep
while the peepers peep
and the bull frogs' bass
is booming deep

in the perfumed light
of a hot summer night
when the full moon calls
and passions ignite?

Come, join me on
the shadowed lawn,
we'll listen to stars,
chat with the dawn,

and watch the sun rise
in each other's eyes,
as morning swims
across the skies.

MOONLIGHT

Was it your mother's idea
to feed you on the moonlight
and frosted stars? It's far
to climb when you grow hungry.
Let a slice of the earth,
with its yesterdays
and its generations,
fill you up and pass
through to its tomorrows.
Your children's children will find
that same moon in a pond
and drink it all one night.

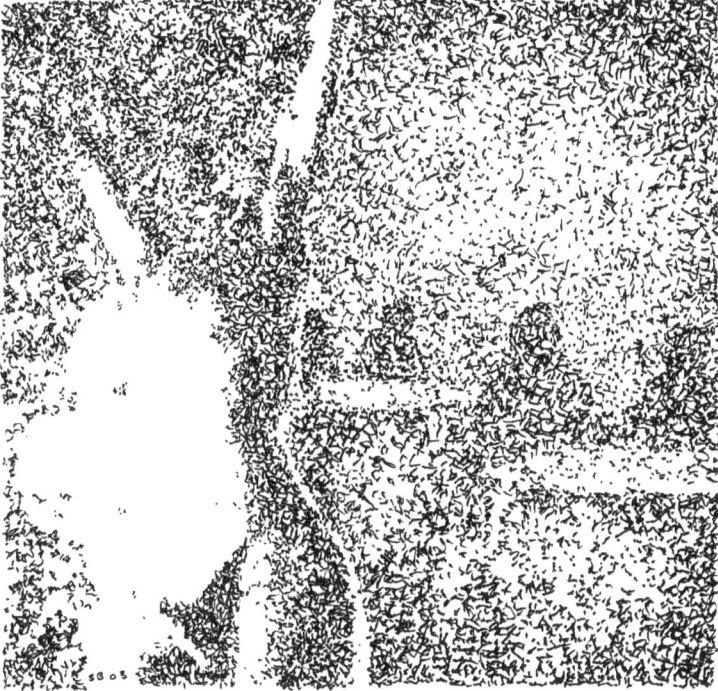

ONE BLUE CAN

Dim-lit room with
one blue can spilling
its mood on you as
smoke curls from
a dozen cigarettes,
glowing eyes in the corners
of forgetfulness.

Nude but never
naked, you wear your
face like a
chastity belt, hard
as the cocks a zipper's
distance from
each lap dance.

cont.

Next week, a different
body wears your
face and we won't
notice you or
the tracks on your
arms as we feed
you small bills.

We came here to
be strangers, babe,
to keep from caring
about you or
ourselves in this
dim-lit room with
one blue can.

What Wind

What wind's a-whistlin' in my ear;
is that time rushin' by, I hear?
It moves too fast—or is it I
who's hurryin', not askin' why?

What wind's a-cuttin' through my life,
what cold and sharp, well-whetted knife?
Some morrow it will slice too deep
and wind will carry me to sleep.

What wind's a-tossin' 'round the days,
like fallen leaves, to go their ways?
That wind, I fear, will howl and rave
until I'm lyin' in my grave.

What is that whistlin' in my ears?
It is the passin' of the years.

OF DREAMS

I am
and always will be
a dreamer

of dreams
too large for my life
to hold

of dreams
that overflow
and run

into
the past as I
grow old

cont.

of dreams
someone will ask
to share

then toss
aside when all
is told

I turn
my collar against
the wind

to dream
alone through life
is cold

DRUM

My heart, it is a drum,
beating wildly,
beating lonely,
through the empty night.
Primal rhythms,
jungle rhythms,
echo in the dark.
Who will dance?
Who will dance?

A Poem Before Breakfast

Now, I'm an early riser—
used to be, I'd sleep in,
stay out late.
But I see more clearly
in the hour before sunrise
and sometimes pour a poem
with my first cup of tea,
finishing it off with a scone.

YOU, WHO ONCE MORE BRIGHTLY SHONE

You have drifted from my heart,
On your separate, silent way;
Though I had hoped, of all I've known,
You, at least, might stay.

There is come an empty place,
Where your memory long lay;
When young, we promised not to part—
"Friends for life," we'd say.

You, who once more brightly shone,
Grow now fainter, day by day;
I can no longer see your face:
Time has dimmed your ray.

On Turning Fifty

We're not young forever;
Be content, I'm told,
And grow old gracefully.
Accept your body,
Love yourself for who you are.

Be content;
Yet only discontent contents me.
My desire keeps me alive,
As I seek still
To fuse with the ideal.

I remain a man in love
With what can be,
What I can make of me;
A man in love with dreams,
An artist of the will.

Time, I know, waits not:
We all go down.
But I'll not fall so easily;
To struggle is to win,
Even when we lose.

STOP BY MY HOUSE

Stop by my house, once more, before you go,
And we shall talk a while of things that were;
There's comfort to be found in things we know.

The time has not yet come that I must grieve,
A day when I shall not see you again;
Stop by my house, once more, before you leave.

For I would sit with you, old friend, although
We may but share a drink, a toast farewell;
Stop by my house, once more, before you go.